PRAYERSCRIPTS
Speaking God's Word Back to Him

"BRETHREN, PRAY FOR US"

SHEPHERDS AFTER MY HEART

31 Days of Prophetic Intercession for

RAISING GODLY SHEPHERDS AND FLOCKS AFTER GOD'S OWN HEART

CYRIL OPOKU

Shepherds After My Heart: 31 Days of Prophetic Intercession for Raising Godly Shepherds and Flocks After God's Own Heart

Published by *Quest Publications*

ISBN: 978-1-988439-87-7

Cover design by *Quest Publications (questpublications@outlook.com)*

Unless otherwise indicated, all Scripture quotations are taken from the World English Bible WEB, which is in the public domain. For more information, visit: www.worldenglish.bible

This book is a work of devotional encouragement. It is not intended to replace biblical study, pastoral counsel, or professional therapy.

Printed in the United States of America.

First Edition: September 2025

For more books like this, visit *PrayerScripts:* https://prayerscripts.org

CONTENTS

Contents..iii

Dedication...v

Preface...vi

How to Use This Book...viii

Introduction..xi

WEEK 1: PRAYING FOR SCATTERED SHEEP..1

Day 1:   Scattered Sheep Gathered..3

Day 2:   Compassion for the Multitudes..5

Day 3:   Protection for the Shepherd...7

Day 4:   Guard Against Offences...9

Day 5:   One Fold, One Shepherd...11

Day 6:   Returning to the Shepherd...13

Day 7:   Turn Back to Zion..15

Day 8:   Perfecting Through the Covenant..17

WEEK 2: EXPOSING THIEVES AND ROBBERS..19

Day 9:   Guardians of the Fold...21

Day 10:   Eyes Open, Hearts Alert...23

Day 11:   Judgment Upon Idol Shepherds...25

Day 12:   Correcting the Shepherds..27

Day 13:   Marking the Deceivers...29

Day 14:   False Ministers Revealed...31

Day 15:   Stopping the Covetous...33

Day 16:   Swift Judgment, Divine Justice...35

Day 17:   Rebuking the Way of Balaam...37

WEEK 3: RAISING SHEPHERDS AFTER GOD'S HEART................................39

Day 18:   Send Laborers, Lord...41

Day 19:   Good Shepherd's Sacrifice...43

Day 20:   Divinely Appointed Leader..45

Day 21:   Pastors After God's Heart..47

Day 22:   Elders with Ready Minds...49

Day 23:   Shepherd Who Seeks... 51

Day 24:   Shepherd's Provision 53

Day 25:   Tender Shepherd 55

WEEK 4: EMPOWERING AND PROTECTING SHEPHERDS 57

Day 26:   Faithful Shepherds of Israel................................. 59

Day 27:   Guardians of the Flock.. 61

Day 28:   Enduring in the Ministry...................................... 63

Day 29:   Holy Leadership Exemplified 65

Day 30:   Christ-Centered Teaching 67

Day 31:   Wise Stewardship 69

    Epilogue 71

    Encourage Others with Your Story............................ 73

    More from PrayerScripts... 74

DEDICATION

This book is lovingly and prayerfully dedicated to the pastors who have shaped my Christian journey in ways words can scarcely capture:

To **REV. (RTD) FRANCIS NYARKO**—it was under your preaching that I first heard the voice of Christ calling me. Your unwavering passion for souls and your faithful oversight laid the foundation of my walk with God. Through your ministry, I learned not only to know the Lord but also to serve His church with reverence and joy.

To **the late REV. JOSEPH OSEI-AMOAH**—your mentorship marked a turning point in my life. You saw potential in me long before I saw it in myself. Under your guidance, I stepped into church leadership for the first time and began the journey of ministerial training. Though you have joined the cloud of witnesses, your legacy of faith and discipleship continues to live on in me.

To **REV. ISAAC DE-GRAFT TAKYI**—you opened my eyes to the spiritual gift of leadership and were the first to commission me to serve as a pastor. Your belief in me, your encouragement, and your push toward deeper theological study have forever shaped my calling and ministry path.

This work is a tribute to your spiritual labor, love, and lasting impact on my life.

PREFACE

"Brethren, pray for us."— 1 Thessalonians 5:25 WEB

From the earliest days of my walk with the Lord, I have been keenly aware of the vital role shepherds play in the life of God's people. Pastors, ministers, elders, and spiritual leaders are more than teachers—they are protectors, guides, and watchmen appointed by God to guard His flock. Yet, even the strongest shepherds face trials, attacks, and moments of weariness. I have seen firsthand the weight of responsibility upon their shoulders, the subtle attacks of the enemy, and the loneliness that often accompanies leadership. It is this awareness that has stirred a deep burden in my heart to intercede, not only for my own pastor but for all who have been called to shepherd God's people faithfully.

Shepherds After My Heart was born out of a desire to cultivate a prophetic culture of prayer over those who lead. This book is a journey of intercession that invites you to step into the heavenly courts on behalf of pastors and ministers around the world. Each day, you will lift your voice to God with Scriptures that anchor your prayers, prophetic declarations that empower the shepherds, and supplications that seek divine protection, wisdom, and anointing. You are not merely praying words; you are engaging in a spiritual assignment that has eternal consequences for the flock and for the Kingdom of God.

Throughout this book, you will encounter prayers that cover the full spectrum of pastoral needs—from protection against spiritual and physical attack, to empowerment in teaching and leadership, to the raising of new shepherds after God's own heart. You will see the global Church as God sees it: as a beloved flock that requires oversight, care, and constant intercession.

It is my hope and prayer that as you move through these 31 days, your sensitivity to the needs of shepherds will deepen, your burden for the Church will intensify, and your faith will rise in confidence that your prayers are making a tangible difference. May every pastor, every minister, and every leader under your intercession be strengthened, protected, and empowered to shepherd with integrity, courage, and divine wisdom.

This book is a labor of love and a call to action. May you be blessed as you step into the ministry of intercession, and may the Lord honor your prayers in ways beyond what your eyes can see.

In Jesus' name, Amen.

In Service of the Chief Shepherd,
Cyril O. *(Toronto, September 2025)*

How to Use This Book

This book is designed as a daily companion to guide you into a prophetic lifestyle of prayer. This is a prayer journey meant to position you to walk in the fullness of God's promises. Here's how to make the most of it:

1. Dedicate a Daily Time:

Set aside a consistent time each day to engage with the prayer for that day. Treat this as sacred time with God, where distractions are minimized, and your heart is fully focused on communion with Him. Ten to twenty minutes daily is sufficient to meditate on the Scripture, pray, and receive revelation.

2. Begin with Scripture Reflection:

Each day begins with a carefully selected Scripture. Read it slowly, meditate on its meaning, and let the Holy Spirit illuminate how it applies to your life. Allow the Word to penetrate your spirit and prepare you to pray from a place of faith and expectancy.

3. Pray the Guided Prayer:

Use the prayer provided as a framework, allowing it to resonate with your own words and personal circumstances. Speak each declaration with authority and confidence, fully believing that God is at work. You may also pause to personalize the prayer for your specific family, career, or ministry needs.

- **Make It Personal**

  These prayers are written in the first person so you can make them your own. Speak them aloud, inserting the names of your family members, your workplace, your church, or your city where applicable. The more you personalize the prayer, the more you will sense its power shaping your reality.

- **Pray with Authority**

  These are not timid requests; they are bold decrees. Lift your voice as a covenant child of God, covered by the blood of Jesus and backed by heaven's authority. When you pray, do so with confidence that Christ has already won the victory on your behalf.

- **Leave Room for the Holy Spirit**

  These written prayers are a guide, not a limit. As you pray, pause to listen. The Holy Spirit may give you prophetic words, insights, or specific instructions. Follow His lead. Allow Him to expand the prayer, add declarations, or guide you into deeper intercession.

4. Journal Your Insights:

Keep a notebook or journal to record any thoughts, revelations, or confirmations you receive during prayer. Writing down what God speaks to you helps solidify understanding and creates a record of breakthrough and growth over time.

5. Repeat as Needed:

Some prayers or themes may need to be revisited multiple times. Answer to prayer is progressive; the more you engage with these prayers in faith, the greater the manifestation in your life and household. You can return to this book at any season to reinforce your victory and dominion.

6. Live in Expectancy:

Prayer is only one part of walking in enlargement—your actions, faith, and obedience amplify the power of these prayers. Move boldly into opportunities, embrace the doors God opens, and live with a confident expectation that God is answering your prayer beyond what you can see or imagine.

By following this guide daily, you will cultivate a lifestyle of prayer and kingdom impact. Let this book be your companion as you step into the new dimensions God has destined for you.

INTRODUCTION

The heartbeat of God's Kingdom is shepherded by those He calls to lead, protect, and guide His people. Yet, every pastor, minister, and spiritual leader faces challenges that are often unseen by the flock they serve. Attacks, spiritual fatigue, false counsel, and the weight of responsibility threaten even the most faithful shepherds. This book is designed to take you beyond casual prayer into intentional, prophetic intercession for the shepherds who carry the mantle of God's people.

Shepherds After My Heart is a spiritual journey. Over the course of 31 days, you will engage in deep, Spirit-led intercession that moves beyond surface-level petitions. You will learn to pray with authority, alignment, and passion for the lives, ministries, and protection of pastors and ministers across the globe. Each day presents a Scripture-based prayer that is designed to ignite both revelation and compassion, equipping you to stand in the gap for those who shepherd God's flock.

As you move through this book, you will experience four progressive layers of intercession. You will begin by praying for scattered and vulnerable sheep, recognizing God's compassion and His desire to restore unity. Next, you will confront the schemes of false shepherds, thieves, and robbers, praying for discernment, justice, and protection. The journey continues with intercession for God to raise up shepherds after His own heart—leaders who embody care, integrity, and courage. Finally, you will pray for the empowerment, protection, and spiritual growth of shepherds to faithfully oversee their flocks, ensuring their ministries thrive and bear eternal fruit.

Expect this book to sharpen your spiritual perception, deepen your love for the Church, and expand your intercessory capacity. Each prayer is crafted to inspire boldness, conviction, and a prophetic voice that calls heaven to action. By the end of these 31 days, you will not only have prayed for shepherds—you will have partnered with God in shaping the spiritual landscape of His Church.

Step into this journey with faith, expectation, and a willing heart. The Lord is inviting you to stand in the gap for His shepherds, and your prayers will make a difference.

WEEK 1: PRAYING FOR SCATTERED SHEEP

Have you ever seen a flock of sheep left unattended on a hillside, wandering aimlessly, vulnerable to every danger? This is the picture Scripture paints of God's people when shepherds fail or when guidance is lacking. Scattered, weary, and often confused, many believers wander from the safety of God's fold, exposed to spiritual attacks and prone to losing their way. Yet, the heart of our God beats with compassion for every wandering soul. He desires not that any should be lost but that every sheep finds rest, direction, and protection under the tender care of shepherds after His own heart.

This week, our prayers focus on interceding for those who are scattered—whether spiritually, emotionally, or physically—and for the shepherds who have the call to bring them back into safety and unity. We are not merely praying for visible leadership, but for divine oversight, guidance, and a shepherding spirit filled with discernment, mercy, and courage. Each PrayerScript this week will awaken your heart to see the needs of the flock through God's eyes, cultivating in you a deep burden for unity and restoration.

We will lift up pastors, ministers, and spiritual leaders, asking God to fill them with unwavering compassion for those who wander. We will declare that the scattered sheep are gathered, that those who have been overlooked are noticed, and that every lost soul is returned to the fold. We pray for divine strategies that restore broken connections and heal the wounds caused by neglect or spiritual attack. This is a week to intercede boldly, declaring that no sheep will remain unguarded, no soul forgotten, and that God's mercy will draw all hearts to Himself. By the end of this week, expect a renewed vision for God's flock and a fresh sensitivity to His compassion for the lost.

DAY 1

SCATTERED SHEEP GATHERED

I saw all Israel scattered upon the hills, as sheep that have
not a shepherd: and the LORD said, These have no master:
let them return every man to his house in peace.
— 1 Kings 22:17 WEB

O Sovereign Shepherd of Israel, I lift up my voice in fervent
intercession, declaring Your mercy over the pastors You have
appointed. I declare that no flock under their care shall remain
scattered or abandoned. Lord, let Your presence move mightily to
gather every wandering sheep, returning them to safety, peace, and
the fold of Your love.

Almighty God, strengthen my pastor with divine wisdom,
discernment, and courage, that he may see every sheep that is lost
or vulnerable. Let him not grow weary in seeking those who are
scattered, but let Your Spirit guide him with understanding,
tenderness, and unwavering commitment.

Father, extend this protection over all ministers of the Gospel
globally. Let Your flock be united under shepherds who act as Your
true representatives, carrying Your heart and compassion to those
who are spiritually weak or misled. May the hands of the wicked be
powerless to divide or scatter Your people.

O Great Shepherd, let Your peace descend upon every
congregation, saturating hearts and minds with faith, obedience,
and love. Restore the weary, strengthen the faint, and let every

wandering soul hear the voice of their shepherd calling them back to Your fold.

Lord, I declare divine alignment and unity in the Church worldwide. Every shepherd, whether local or remote, shall be clothed with Your authority and grace to lead, protect, and nurture Your flock. Let no one stray beyond the reach of Your mercy and power.

In Jesus' name, Amen.

DAY 2

COMPASSION FOR THE MULTITUDES

But when he saw the multitudes, he was moved with compassion on them, because they fainted, and were scattered abroad, as sheep having no shepherd.
— Matthew 9:36 WEB

O Compassionate Lord, I come before You with a heart burdened for the sheep that faint and wander. I call upon Your Spirit to fill my pastor with the same compassion that moved Jesus toward the scattered multitudes. Let his heart burn for every lost soul, his eyes open to the hidden hurts, and his hands ready to lift those who are weary.

Father, breathe Your compassion into all ministers of the Gospel. Let them walk in the footsteps of the Good Shepherd, seeking the hurting, comforting the broken, and guiding the confused back to paths of righteousness. Let no sheep remain neglected or overlooked under their watch.

Almighty God, shield Your shepherds from distraction, pride, or spiritual fatigue. Strengthen their endurance, refresh their hearts daily, and provide divine strategies to rescue the wandering and protect the fold. Let Your compassion overflow through them into the lives of many.

O Lord, let the scattered find sanctuary in Your truth and the shepherds You have raised. May revival of heart, vision, and mission spread through every church, lifting the fainting and strengthening the weak. Make Your ministers bold yet tender, wise yet gentle, as they shepherd Your flock.

Father, I decree an outpouring of Your Spirit upon all who lead Your people. Let Your mercy, guidance, and power accompany every step they take, turning despair into hope, confusion into clarity, and weakness into strength.

In Jesus' name, Amen.

DAY 3

PROTECTION FOR THE SHEPHERD

> Awake, O sword, against my shepherd, and against the man that is my fellow, saith the LORD of hosts: smite the shepherd, and the sheep shall be scattered: and I will turn mine hand upon the little ones.
> — Zechariah 13:7 WEB

O Mighty Protector, I lift up my pastor to You, the Defender of Your chosen servants. I declare a hedge of fire and a shield of angels around him, preserving him from every attack that seeks to scatter the flock. Let every weapon formed against him and against other ministers of the Gospel be rendered powerless and turn back upon the enemy.

Lord, preserve the shepherd from temptation, betrayal, and any form of spiritual sabotage. Strengthen his resolve, sharpen his discernment, and grant him courage to stand firm even when adversaries rise against him. Let Your hand cover the little ones, the vulnerable, and the spiritually weak under his care.

Almighty God, extend this protection over all pastors and ministers worldwide. Let Your Spirit guard their hearts, minds, and ministries, making them immovable in righteousness and steadfast in truth. Let Your justice fall upon those who would harm the shepherds or the flock.

Father, fortify the ministry of every shepherd with divine insight and supernatural favor. Let their teachings bring life, their prayers bring healing, and their counsel bring restoration. May Your anointing repel every attack and secure the flock in unity, peace, and faith.

Lord, I declare that no power of darkness shall cause Your sheep to be scattered. Let Your glory manifest through every shepherd as they lead with Your heart, love with Your mercy, and protect with Your strength.

In Jesus' name, Amen.

DAY 4

GUARD AGAINST OFFENCES

And Jesus said to them, All of you shall be offended because of me this night: for it is written, I will strike the shepherd, and the sheep shall be scattered.
— Mark 14:27 WEB

O Faithful Lord, I intercede for my pastor, declaring that no offence shall prevail to weaken his ministry or scatter the flock. Let every plot, betrayal, and divisive act be exposed and nullified by Your Spirit. Strengthen him to stand unshakable in integrity and steadfast in love.

Father, I lift all ministers of the Gospel into Your hands, asking that You protect them from every snare designed to cause offence or disunity. Let their hearts be filled with resilience, wisdom, and discernment to navigate every trial with grace.

Mighty God, replace the potential confusion and disappointment with Your clarity and peace. Let every attack that targets the shepherds serve only to refine them, increase their faith, and strengthen the bond with their flock.

Lord, raise the hearts of Your sheep to recognize the voice of their shepherd and remain unshaken amidst adversity. Let reconciliation, love, and unity flow through every congregation, guided by those You have appointed.

Father, I decree that every ministry under Your call shall flourish. Let Your favor protect every shepherd, multiply their influence, and preserve the flock from scattering or harm.

In Jesus' name, Amen.

DAY 5

ONE FOLD, ONE SHEPHERD

And other sheep I have, which are not of this fold: them
also I must bring, and they shall hear my voice; and there
shall be one fold, and one shepherd.
— John 10:16 WEB

O Good Shepherd of all flocks, I lift up my pastor and all ministers of the Gospel, declaring that Your voice shall be heard clearly by every scattered and lost soul. Unite the diverse sheep under one shepherd, one vision, and one heart, bringing cohesion, understanding, and divine alignment.

Father, grant my pastor supernatural wisdom to reach those outside the fold, extending Your kingdom with love, truth, and compassion. Let the flock hear his voice in harmony with Your Spirit, and follow without confusion or fear.

Lord, raise a global army of shepherds who will operate with Your heart and care, shepherding Your scattered sheep with passion, diligence, and integrity. Let Your unity be evident in every ministry, congregation, and community of believers.

Mighty God, protect every minister from division, rivalry, and misunderstanding. Let Your Spirit guide their decisions, strengthen their teaching, and multiply their influence in drawing souls to Christ.

Father, I decree Your glory over every shepherd and every flock worldwide. Let Your name be honored through their ministry, Your purposes fulfilled, and Your kingdom advanced in power and love. In Jesus' name, Amen.

DAY 6

RETURNING TO THE SHEPHERD

For you were as sheep going astray, but are now returned
to the Shepherd and Bishop of your souls.
— 1 Peter 2:25 WEB

O Lord, the Great Shepherd and Bishop of our souls, I lift up my
pastor and all ministers, declaring restoration, guidance, and divine
wisdom upon their hearts. May they shepherd their flocks with
diligence, courage, and tender care, bringing back those who have
wandered into Your fold.

Father, strengthen my pastor to discern every lost sheep, protect
them from danger, and guide them with Your voice and direction.
Let him lead with both authority and compassion, embodying the
heart of Christ in every interaction.

Almighty God, extend this grace over all pastors and leaders of the
Church globally. Let Your Spirit empower them to rescue the
wandering, restore the weak, and uphold the integrity of Your
ministry.

Lord, let every sheep hear Your voice through Your shepherds. May
hearts be softened, lives transformed, and souls restored to
fellowship, obedience, and faith. Let Your peace reign over every
congregation, filling them with hope, joy, and unity.

Father, I declare supernatural protection, wisdom, and favor over
every minister of the Gospel. Let them faithfully lead Your people,

guiding them back to You, the true Shepherd of all. In Jesus' name, Amen.

DAY 7

TURN BACK TO ZION

My people have been lost sheep; their shepherds have caused them to go astray, they have turned them away on the mountains; they have gone from mountain to hill, they have forgotten their resting place.
— Jeremiah 50:6 WEB

O Gracious Father, I intercede for my pastor and all ministers, praying that Your Spirit will bring every lost sheep under their care back from confusion, error, and wandering. Restore the scattered, refresh the weary, and let Your flock remember their true resting place in You.

Lord, reveal Yourself anew to every shepherd, igniting their passion for guidance, protection, and restoration of the flock. Let them lead with Your wisdom, understanding, and strength, securing Your sheep from harm and distraction.

Father, empower all ministers to rise above worldly pressures, selfish ambition, and spiritual fatigue. Let them shepherd Your people with integrity, vigilance, and divine insight, so that no sheep is left vulnerable or abandoned.

Mighty God, restore every flock with unity, faith, and hope, ensuring that Your kingdom expands through faithful shepherds. Let Your glory shine through every pastoral ministry, bringing light to those who have lost their way.

Lord, I declare that Your flock shall return to their resting place, guided by shepherds after Your heart, protected, nurtured, and firmly established in Your truth and love.

In Jesus' name, Amen.

DAY 8

PERFECTING THROUGH THE COVENANT

> Now the God of peace, who brought again from the dead our Lord Jesus, that great shepherd of the sheep, through the blood of the everlasting covenant, Make you perfect in every good work to do his will, working in you that which is well-pleasing in his sight, through Jesus Christ; to whom be glory for ever and ever. Amen.
> — Hebrews 13:20-21 WEB

O Eternal Shepherd, I lift up my pastor and all ministers, asking that through the blood of the everlasting covenant, You perfect them in every good work, enabling them to fulfill Your will with excellence, grace, and diligence.

Father, strengthen their hearts, minds, and spirits to shepherd faithfully, protecting the flock, feeding the hungry, and restoring the weak. Let their ministries reflect Your glory and advance Your kingdom on earth.

Almighty God, grant supernatural wisdom and discernment to all ministers worldwide, helping them to carry out every assignment according to Your perfect plan. May Your Spirit guide their steps, multiply their efforts, and shield them from every adversary seeking to disrupt Your work.

Lord, let the anointing of the great Shepherd empower them to nurture Your flock with understanding, mercy, and truth. Let their lives exemplify integrity, humility, and obedience, inspiring others to follow You wholeheartedly.

Father, I declare that every shepherd raised in Your name shall accomplish their divine calling, perfected in every good work, and fully pleasing in Your sight. Let Your glory shine through every ministry, transforming lives and drawing souls to You.

In Jesus' name, Amen.

WEEK 2: EXPOSING THIEVES AND ROBBERS

The enemy often comes in subtle ways, cloaked in the appearance of righteousness. False shepherds, thieves, and robbers move among the flock with destructive intentions, seeking to steal, kill, and scatter. These are leaders and influences who may disguise greed, ambition, or selfishness as spiritual authority. This week, our prayers will confront deception with discernment, injustice with the righteousness of God, and danger with divine protection. We are interceding not only for the exposed sheep but also for the Church as a whole, asking the Lord to reveal hidden snares and guard His people.

As you enter this week of prayer, prepare your heart for revelation and clarity. Pray for God to expose those whose leadership leads to division, confusion, or harm. Declare that the schemes of thieves and robbers are frustrated and that their influence is nullified in the name of Jesus. We will lift up pastors, elders, and ministers, asking for supernatural protection over their ministries, reputations, and families. Pray that God would grant wisdom to discern false teaching and courage to confront injustice with grace and truth.

The Scriptures this week remind us that the flock is precious to God and that He will not leave it defenseless. As you intercede, visualize the Church shielded by His Spirit, secure in His guidance, and free from manipulation or exploitation. Pray for leaders to be strengthened in integrity, for communities to be rooted in truth, and for the harvest of souls to remain intact despite the schemes of the enemy. By the end of this week, you will walk in heightened spiritual awareness and see God's protection over His flock manifest in new and powerful ways.

DAY 9

GUARDIANS OF THE FOLD

"Truly, truly, I tell you, the one who doesn't enter by the door into the sheepfold, but climbs up another way, that one is a thief and a robber. But the one who enters by the door is the shepherd of the sheep. I am the door; whoever enters through me will be saved, and will go in and out, and find pasture. The thief comes only to steal, kill, and destroy; I came that they may have life, and have it abundantly."
— John 10:1-2, 9-10 WEB

O Sovereign Lord, Eternal Shepherd of the righteous, I rise today to intercede with a heart ablaze for Your ministers. Father, I declare over my pastor and all shepherds of Your flock that no thief, robber, or deceitful hand will succeed in stealing the souls You have entrusted to them. By Your Spirit, protect them from every subtle attack that seeks to disrupt, divide, or destroy the harvest of their labors. Let Your divine strategy shield their calling from the schemes of the enemy.

Heavenly Father, expose every false teacher and deceiver that lurks among the fold, and let their plans come to nothing. Strengthen the spiritual discernment of every shepherd so that they may recognize wolves in sheep's clothing before harm comes. Let integrity, wisdom, and godly vigilance be their constant companions. Empower them to stand boldly in truth, preaching the life-giving Word without compromise or fear.

O Great Shepherd, I pray that Your pastors and ministers experience the abundant life You promised. Fill them with supernatural joy, peace, and the unshakable assurance of Your presence as they labor in the vineyard. Restore energy where weariness threatens, and renew passion for the lost and the scattered. Surround them with faithful helpers who amplify their calling and protect the flock in unity.

Father, let every attempt by thieves, greed-driven leaders, or malicious forces to corrupt or exploit Your flock be frustrated and nullified. Let Your righteous judgment fall swiftly upon those who seek to harm Your laborers. Strengthen the hearts of Your shepherds so that they may shepherd with courage, compassion, and unwavering faithfulness, leaving no sheep unattended.

I declare, Lord, that the global church is preserved under the watchful eyes of godly leaders raised according to Your heart. Let the light of Your Word penetrate every corner of darkness, bringing salvation and protection to all Your children. May Your ministers walk in wisdom, courage, and the authority of heaven, defeating every plan of destruction in their path.

In Jesus' name, Amen.

DAY 10

EYES OPEN, HEARTS ALERT

"The watchmen are blind, they are all ignorant, they are all silent dogs; they cannot bark. They are greedy dogs that cannot have enough, shepherds that cannot understand; they all look to their own way, everyone for his gain, from his quarter."
— Isaiah 56:10-11 WEB

O Almighty God, Eternal King and Judge of all the earth, I stand in the gap for the shepherds of Your global Church. Lord, open the eyes of Your servants so that they do not sleep in spiritual ignorance or turn deaf to the cries of the needy. Remove all blindness from those who guide Your people and grant them supernatural understanding. May they not grow weary or distracted by personal gain, but remain vigilant, faithful, and wholly devoted to the flock entrusted to their care.

Father, I decree that every greed-driven and self-serving leader be exposed, and that Your flock is safeguarded from their destructive influence. Raise up shepherds after Your own heart, men and women of integrity who feed the hungry, heal the broken, and seek the wandering with tender care. Let Your Spirit empower every minister to act with wisdom, discernment, and courage in the face of challenges.

O Lord of Hosts, guard Your pastors against spiritual complacency and apathy. Strengthen them to remain watchful and alert, guarding the fold with diligence and humility. Replace selfish motives with pure devotion, and may their lives be a testimony of obedience and selfless service.

Almighty Shepherd, protect the global church from leaders who seek to enrich themselves while neglecting their responsibility. Let every scheme of the enemy be thwarted, and let justice and righteousness prevail among Your servants. Empower Your ministers to shepherd with understanding and to lead with hearts aligned to Your will.

Father, bring unity and holiness to Your Church through faithful shepherds. Let the light of Your Word shine through their lives, dispelling ignorance, revealing truth, and guiding Your children into the abundance of Your Kingdom. May every shepherd faithfully represent Your heart in all that they do.

In Jesus' name, Amen.

DAY 11

JUDGMENT UPON IDOL SHEPHERDS

"Woe to the idol shepherd that leaves the flock! The sword shall be upon his arm, and upon his right eye; his arm shall be completely dried up, and his right eye shall be utterly darkened."
— Zechariah 11:17 WEB

O Righteous Judge, Supreme Shepherd of Israel, I lift my voice in fervent intercession for Your ministers worldwide. Lord, expose every idol shepherd who abandons the flock for selfish gain. Let their power, influence, and schemes crumble under the weight of Your justice. Protect the hearts of faithful pastors from being deceived or swayed by such leaders. May Your sword of truth strike every corruption and hypocrisy that seeks to harm Your people.

Father, I declare preservation and divine guidance over my pastor and every faithful servant of Yours. Strengthen them to shepherd with courage and purity, guarding the flock with integrity. Let their eyes see clearly and their hands remain strong to perform acts of mercy, healing, and spiritual provision. May they never be ensnared by the allure of prestige or riches, but stand firmly as vessels of Your righteousness.

O God, pour wisdom into their councils and understanding into their hearts. Let every shepherd who walks after Your heart be a beacon of hope, guiding the scattered sheep back into safety. Let

Your Spirit protect them from attacks, slander, and manipulation, ensuring the fold is not left defenseless.

Almighty Shepherd, let every idol shepherd be judged swiftly according to Your righteousness, and may Your faithful ministers be strengthened to advance Your Kingdom. Let justice flow through Your Church, restoring peace and security for the lost and vulnerable.

I proclaim that Your servants shall rise in power, courage, and divine favor, fulfilling the call You have placed upon them. Let Your glory rest upon Your faithful shepherds, and let Your Word guide every decision they make for the good of the flock.

In Jesus' name, Amen.

DAY 12

CORRECTING THE SHEPHERDS

"Son of man, prophesy against the shepherds of Israel; prophesy, and say to them, 'Thus says the Lord GOD to the shepherds: Woe to the shepherds of Israel who feed themselves! Should not the shepherds feed the flocks? You eat the fat, and you clothe yourselves with the wool; you kill the fattened sheep, but you do not feed the flock. You have not strengthened the weak, healed the sick, bound up the broken, brought back the driven away, sought the lost, but with force and cruelty have ruled them. And they were scattered, because there was no shepherd; and they became food for all the beasts of the field when they were scattered.'"
— Ezekiel 34:2-5 WEB

O Great Shepherd, I cry out on behalf of Your ministers and the global Church. Lord, correct the shepherds who feed themselves while neglecting Your flock. Let their hearts be turned from selfish gain to selfless service. Protect the faithful shepherds from being overshadowed by greed-driven leaders, and let their ministries flourish according to Your purpose. Strengthen them to shepherd with mercy, compassion, and diligence.

Father, restore health to every minister who is weary or burdened. Heal the sick, bind up the broken, and seek diligently those who are lost and scattered. Let Your Spirit empower them to shepherd as You have instructed, feeding the flock with wisdom, love, and understanding. Let Your hand guide every step they take, so that Your people are protected, nurtured, and united.

Almighty God, remove force, cruelty, and oppression from those who rule selfishly. Let their deeds be brought into the light and judged according to Your justice. Raise up shepherds who care deeply for the weak, advocate for the helpless, and labor to restore the lost. Let Your glory shine through their actions, drawing many to Your Kingdom.

O Lord, I decree that no sheep shall remain scattered under the care of faithful ministers. Protect every flock from wolves, imposters, and selfish rulers. Let Your faithful servants rise as examples of Your heart, demonstrating the character of Christ in every act of leadership.

May Your Church be led by shepherds who seek Your will above all, guiding the flock into abundant life, protection, and provision. Let every faithful minister fulfill their calling without fear, corruption, or compromise.

In Jesus' name, Amen.

DAY 13

MARKING THE DECEIVERS

"Now I appeal to you, brothers, to watch those who cause divisions and offenses, contrary to the teaching you learned; avoid them. For such people do not serve our Lord Christ, but their own appetites, and by smooth talk and flattery they deceive the hearts of the naive."
— Romans 16:17-18 WEB

O Lord of Truth, Eternal Judge and Protector of Your Church, I lift up Your ministers before Your throne today. Father, mark those who cause divisions and offenses in Your Church, those who seek to deceive Your flock through flattery, selfish motives, or cunning words. Let their schemes be exposed and neutralized by Your Spirit. Protect my pastor and all faithful leaders from being harmed or misled by these deceivers.

Mighty God, strengthen the discernment of every shepherd so that they can detect hidden agendas and manipulations. Fill them with wisdom and boldness to confront false teachers and uphold the integrity of Your Word. Let every attempt at deception fail, and let Your Church remain unified under godly leadership.

Father, preserve the hearts of Your ministers from discouragement and spiritual attack. Empower them to shepherd with vigilance, courage, and unwavering faith, providing care and guidance to all entrusted to them. Let Your Spirit guide every decision and action, bringing justice and righteousness to Your Church.

Almighty Shepherd, raise up faithful laborers who speak truth, correct error, and protect the flock from cunning and deceit. Let Your Word be the lamp and shield for every pastor, ensuring Your Church flourishes and Your name is glorified in every act of ministry.

Lord, I decree that Your Church is protected, Your ministers are empowered, and every deceiver is exposed and judged according to Your righteousness. Let Your glory and authority rest upon Your shepherds as they faithfully serve Your Kingdom.

In Jesus' name, Amen.

DAY 14

FALSE MINISTERS REVEALED

"For such men are false apostles, deceitful workers, disguising themselves as apostles of Christ. And no wonder! For Satan himself disguises himself as an angel of light. So it is no surprise if his servants also disguise themselves as servants of righteousness. Their end will match their deeds."
— 2 Corinthians 11:13-15 WEB

O Eternal God, Supreme Shepherd of Your people, I cry out for the protection and discernment of Your ministers. Father, reveal every false apostle, deceitful worker, and disguised servant of Satan who infiltrates Your Church. Let their schemes be fully exposed and neutralized, and may their influence be broken. Guard my pastor and all faithful leaders from being led astray by clever disguises and hidden agendas.

Lord, equip every shepherd with spiritual discernment and clarity of vision. Let them recognize deception, reject compromise, and stand firmly in Your truth. Fill them with the courage to confront falsehoods, defend the weak, and guide the flock with wisdom. Let integrity, righteousness, and holiness characterize their leadership, protecting the global Church from harm.

O Mighty Shepherd, let the end of all false ministers be according to their works. Bring justice swiftly, and let Your righteous judgment prevail. Strengthen Your faithful servants to shepherd with courage and unwavering commitment to Your Word. Let every deception be uncovered, and let every sheep be guided safely into Your fold.

Father, let Your ministers flourish in the light of Your Spirit, demonstrating Your truth, love, and authority. Protect them from spiritual ambush, empower their ministries, and ensure that the Church thrives under godly leadership. May Your name be glorified in every faithful act of stewardship.

In Jesus' name, Amen.

DAY 15

STOPPING THE COVETOUS

"Whose mouths must be stopped, who subvert whole households, teaching things which they ought not, for filthy lucre's sake."
— Titus 1:11 WEB

O Holy Judge, Righteous Shepherd, I raise a prophetic intercession over my pastor and every faithful minister of Your Word. Father, stop every corrupt teacher who seeks gain through the exploitation of Your flock. Let their mouths be silenced and their plans frustrated. Protect the integrity of Your Church and strengthen every shepherd to lead with purity of heart and devotion to Your Word.

Heavenly Father, pour wisdom, courage, and discernment into every pastor, minister, and overseer. Let them shepherd with transparency and righteousness, refusing to be swayed by greed or selfish motives. Establish them as beacons of truth, integrity, and faithfulness in their ministries. Let Your Spirit guard them against manipulation and exploitation.

O Lord, shield Your Church from harmful doctrines and destructive leaders. Let every covetous heart be exposed and humbled. Strengthen Your faithful ministers to teach, guide, and correct according to Your Word, not for personal gain but for the growth and protection of the flock.

Father, empower Your ministers to shepherd with love, diligence, and discernment. Protect every church from exploitation, deceit, and harm. Let Your Church rise as a holy and unified body, led by shepherds who reflect Your heart and righteousness in all things.

I declare that Your faithful ministers shall prosper in their calling, and Your Church shall be preserved under godly leadership, free from corruption and covetousness.

In Jesus' name, Amen.

DAY 16

SWIFT JUDGMENT, DIVINE JUSTICE

"And through covetousness, they will with false words make merchandise of you; whose judgment, from long ago, has not lingered, and their destruction does not slumber."
— 2 Peter 2:3 WEB

O Righteous Judge, Almighty Shepherd, I intercede for my pastor and all godly ministers across the earth. Father, let every covetous, deceitful servant be swiftly judged and destroyed according to Your justice. Protect Your faithful ministers from the manipulations of those who seek to exploit, enslave, or mislead Your flock. Let their schemes come to nothing in the power of Your Spirit.

Lord, fill every shepherd with boldness and discernment, enabling them to expose falsehood, protect the innocent, and shepherd with integrity. Let Your Word be their sword and Your Spirit their shield against deceit, greed, and corruption. Strengthen their hearts to remain faithful despite challenges and attacks from ungodly leaders.

Almighty God, let Your global Church be preserved and prosper under the care of faithful ministers. Let every plot of destruction, covetousness, or deceit be thwarted and neutralized. Raise up righteous leaders to replace every corrupt figure and restore peace, order, and protection to the flock.

Father, empower Your ministers to teach truth with clarity, shepherd with compassion, and lead with courage. Let Your justice prevail and Your Church rise in holiness, righteousness, and unity.

In Jesus' name, Amen.

DAY 17

REBUKING THE WAY OF BALAAM

"They have eyes full of adultery, and cannot cease from sin; beguiling unstable souls; they have hearts exercised in greed, cursed children, who have forsaken the right way, gone astray, following the way of Balaam, the son of Bosor, who loved the wages of unrighteousness, but he was rebuked for his iniquity: the dumb ass spoke with man's voice and restrained the madness of the prophet."
— 2 Peter 2:14-16 WEB

O Mighty God, Protector of Your flock and Judge of the nations, I stand in the gap for Your ministers and the global Church. Father, rebuke the false shepherds who follow the way of Balaam, led by greed, adultery, and deceit. Let their influence over Your people be nullified, and may Your righteous hand restrain their madness and corruption. Protect my pastor and all faithful ministers from their schemes and manipulations.

Lord, fill Your shepherds with boldness, wisdom, and discernment. Let their eyes see clearly, their hearts remain pure, and their hands be strong to protect and guide the flock. Empower them to shepherd with integrity, exposing deception and restoring the lost to Your fold. May they walk in Your Spirit, guided by Your Word, and strengthened by Your promises.

Father, thwart every plan of covetousness and manipulation. Let the global Church flourish under godly leadership, free from the influence of false prophets and deceitful teachers. Let Your justice and righteousness prevail, bringing stability, peace, and spiritual abundance to every flock.

O Sovereign Shepherd, empower Your ministers to rebuke the wicked boldly, guide the vulnerable wisely, and restore the wandering with compassion. May Your Word be the light and authority that leads all faithful shepherds to triumph over every scheme of the enemy.

In Jesus' name, Amen.

Week 3: Raising Shepherds After God's Heart

True shepherds do not merely occupy a position—they carry a divine calling. They feed the flock, guide the wandering, protect the weak, and lead with a heart aligned to God's own. This week, we lift our voices in intercession, asking God to raise up shepherds after His heart—leaders who will care for the flock with integrity, wisdom, and love. Our prayers focus on calling forth men and women of courage and compassion, who will not shrink from sacrifice but will faithfully fulfill their divine assignments.

As we pray this week, let us declare that God's vision for shepherding is restored in His Church. Pray that pastors, elders, and ministers are aligned with God's heart, equipped with discernment, and empowered to lead effectively. Ask for wisdom to guide their decisions, for grace to endure trials, and for humility that models Christlikeness. Intercede for those who are being prepared in secret, that God's hand would reveal them at the appointed time, ready to shepherd the flock in ways that restore hope, build faith, and foster unity.

We also pray for the existing shepherds who may be weary, wounded, or overwhelmed. Ask God to renew their passion, protect their hearts, and inspire them with a fresh vision for the flock. Declare that the Church will be led by those who feed and not exploit, who guide and do not mislead, and who sacrifice personal comfort for the sake of the Kingdom. By the end of this week, expect a renewed confidence that God is actively raising leaders who reflect His heart, protect His sheep, and advance His Kingdom in power, love, and integrity.

DAY 18

SEND LABORERS, LORD

"Therefore he said to them, The harvest truly is great, but
the laborers are few. Pray therefore the Lord of the harvest,
that he may send out laborers into his harvest."
— Luke 10:2 WEB

O Lord of the Harvest, I lift up Your servants and ask that You send
forth shepherds after Your own heart into every field of Your
vineyard. I declare that Your Church shall not lack leaders who are
diligent, compassionate, and obedient to Your voice. Let every
pastor, every minister of the Gospel, rise in courage and boldness
to gather the harvest of souls with wisdom and grace.

Heavenly Father, empower my pastor and all Your shepherds
worldwide to labor faithfully, without weariness, sowing the seeds
of righteousness, and reaping the fruits of Your Spirit. Strengthen
them with perseverance when trials press hard upon them, and let
Your Spirit continually renew their vision, their zeal, and their love
for the sheep. May no obstacle or distraction divert them from the
calling You have placed upon their lives.

O Great Shepherd, release supernatural strategies to discern and
reach the lost, that no soul will be neglected in Your harvest. Raise
up laborers in alignment with Your heart, those who will lead with
humility, compassion, and courage, reflecting Christ in every word,
every act, and every decision. Let the laborers be many, and let the
harvest abound in every nation, tribe, and tongue.

41

Father, protect the shepherds from discouragement, from those who would oppose them, and from weariness of spirit. Equip them with Your armor, surround them with godly counsel, and let their ministries flourish as testimonies of Your glory. May their lives be living epistles of faithfulness, inspiring all who see them to trust in You.

O Lord, I decree that every minister of the Gospel shall hear Your call clearly, obey Your leading unreservedly, and minister with power and integrity. May Your kingdom expand, and may Your flock be fed with understanding, truth, and love. Raise up shepherds according to Your perfect will, to care for Your people with sacrificial hearts and shepherd's wisdom.

In Jesus' name, Amen.

DAY 19

Good Shepherd's Sacrifice

"I am the good shepherd. The good shepherd lays down his life for the sheep."
— John 10:11-13 WEB

O Eternal Shepherd, I lift before You every pastor, minister, and overseer of Your flock. I declare that they shall walk in the fullness of the good shepherd's heart, laying down their lives daily for the care, protection, and nourishment of the sheep You have entrusted to them. Let their ministries reflect the perfect love of Christ, fearless and unwavering in the face of trials, opposition, or fatigue.

Almighty Father, grant them discernment to guide Your people safely, keeping the wolves of deception and destruction away. Strengthen their hands for every labor, and let their hearts burn with zeal for Your glory. Protect them from the temptation of selfish ambition, that they may serve Your flock faithfully, not for gain, but for the reward of obedience and the joy of seeing souls saved, healed, and restored.

Lord Jesus, may my pastor and all Your ministers feel the weight and privilege of their calling as true shepherds. Give them endurance for the storms, courage in persecution, and wisdom to navigate the complexities of their responsibilities. Let their compassion be genuine, their counsel wise, and their vision aligned perfectly with Your heart.

Gracious God, I prophesy that Your Spirit shall fill them with supernatural strength to lay down personal desires and comforts for the sake of the flock. May they model humility, patience, and sacrificial love in every aspect of their ministry. Let their lives bear witness to Your faithfulness and lead many into the safety of Your fold.

I pray that every shepherd in Your Church shall operate under Your guidance, flowing in the fullness of Your presence, defending, feeding, and nurturing their sheep as Christ did. Let no sheep be lost due to negligence, but all experience the tender care of leaders after Your own heart.

In Jesus' name, Amen.

DAY 20

DIVINELY APPOINTED LEADER

"Moses spoke to the Lord, saying, Let the Lord, the God of the spirits of all flesh, set a man over the congregation, who may go out before them and who may come in before them, who may lead them out and bring them in, that the congregation of the Lord may not be as sheep that have no shepherd."
— Numbers 27:15-17 WEB

O Sovereign God, I lift up all pastors, elders, and church leaders, asking that You divinely appoint shepherds after Your heart to guide Your people. Let every minister be firmly established by Your Spirit, walking in wisdom, discernment, and righteousness as they lead the congregation. May their leadership be a reflection of Your divine authority and tender care.

Almighty Father, release supernatural guidance upon them to lead faithfully, bringing the lost into safety, feeding the flock with Your Word, and protecting them from all harm. May every shepherd be vigilant, courageous, and unwavering, guarding Your people from false doctrines, distractions, and predators that seek to scatter the sheep.

Lord, strengthen their spirits, renew their vision, and inspire them with creativity and wisdom to shepherd effectively in every circumstance. Let them understand Your heart fully, and lead Your people according to Your perfect will. May the flock prosper under their care, and may the leaders be honored for their integrity and faithfulness.

O Eternal Shepherd, protect them from discouragement, weariness, and temptation. Equip them with the armor of Your truth, the shield of faith, and the sword of the Spirit. Let every decision, every step, and every word be guided by Your presence, leading Your people to spiritual safety and abundance.

Father, I decree that Your appointed leaders shall multiply, establishing households of faith, sowing righteousness, and bringing Your glory to every congregation. Let no sheep wander lost, but may every shepherd act as a faithful reflection of Your heart and love.

In Jesus' name, Amen.

DAY 21

PASTORS AFTER GOD'S HEART

"Turn, O backsliding children, says the Lord, for I am
married to you. I will take you from one city, and from two
families I will bring you to Zion. I will give you pastors
according to My heart, who will feed you with knowledge
and understanding."
— Jeremiah 3:14-15 WEB

O Faithful Father, I lift before You every pastor, teacher, and
overseer in Your Church. I proclaim that You shall raise shepherds
after Your own heart, filled with wisdom, knowledge, and
understanding. May these leaders nurture the flock, feeding them
with revelation, teaching, and guidance that glorifies Your name
and strengthens Your kingdom.

Almighty God, I ask that You gather scattered sheep from every
city, town, and village, placing them under shepherds who truly
know Your heart. Let these ministers exhibit compassion, patience,
and discernment, guiding the congregation away from false paths
and into Your truth. May they be living examples of Christ's love,
leading with integrity, humility, and courage.

Lord, endow them with discernment to navigate complex spiritual
landscapes, to correct with gentleness, and to teach with clarity.
Protect them from discouragement, envy, and distraction. Let Your
Spirit continuously renew them, infusing their ministries with

power, anointing, and boldness to proclaim the Word of God faithfully.

Gracious Father, I decree that every flock under their care will flourish, finding rest, direction, and encouragement. Let Your glory shine through Your shepherds, bringing transformation, healing, and revival to every congregation. May the hearts of the ministers and the sheep beat in alignment with Your purposes.

O Lord, let the Church rise with shepherds after Your own heart, who will lead with divine insight, feed the people with understanding, and cultivate righteousness. Let these shepherds shine as beacons of truth, love, and faithful guidance in a world of spiritual hunger.

In Jesus' name, Amen.

DAY 22

ELDERS WITH READY MINDS

"The elders who are among you I exhort, as a fellow elder and a witness of the sufferings of Christ, and partaker of the glory that shall be revealed: Shepherd the flock of God which is among you, exercising oversight, not by constraint, but willingly, not for filthy lucre, but with a ready mind; nor as lording it over God's heritage, but being examples to the flock. And when the chief Shepherd shall appear, you shall receive a crown of glory that fades not away."
— 1 Peter 5:1-4 WEB

O Chief Shepherd of the sheep, I lift up all pastors, elders, and overseers in Your Church. I declare that they shall shepherd the flock willingly, with joy, with hearts full of zeal for Your glory, not for gain, but out of love and dedication. May their ministries be marked by integrity, humility, and diligence, as they exemplify Christ's leadership to the congregation.

Almighty God, give them readiness of mind, steadfast devotion, and unshakable faith to guide Your people through every trial. Let their counsel be wise, their teaching grounded in Your Word, and their hearts attuned to the leading of Your Spirit. Protect them from pride, distractions, and corruption, and fill them with endurance to serve faithfully to the end.

Lord, I pray that Your Spirit continually renews their strength, vision, and insight, enabling them to shepherd effectively, guard the flock, and restore the lost. Let them be shining examples of sacrificial leadership, humble service, and unwavering commitment to Your will.

Gracious Father, may the sheep under their care experience provision, protection, and spiritual growth. Let the elders' influence ripple through families, communities, and nations, bringing revival, transformation, and alignment with Your purposes.

I decree that when the chief Shepherd appears, Your faithful ministers shall receive eternal crowns of glory, their labors fruitful, their hearts rewarded, and their ministries honored before You and all creation.

In Jesus' name, Amen.

DAY 23

SHEPHERD WHO SEEKS

"For thus says the Lord God: Behold, I, even I, will search
for my sheep, and will seek them out."
— Ezekiel 34:11-16 WEB

O Lord God, Eternal Shepherd of Israel, I lift before You every
pastor, every minister, every overseer who bears responsibility for
Your flock. I declare that You shall empower them to seek the lost,
to heal the broken, and to feed the weary with Your Word. May their
hearts beat in perfect alignment with Your desire to restore, protect,
and nurture Your people.

Heavenly Father, fill them with wisdom and discernment to find the
scattered, rescue the oppressed, and restore the weak. Let every
shepherd hear Your voice clearly, follow Your guidance unerringly,
and minister in ways that bring life, hope, and strength to the flock.
Protect them from discouragement, spiritual attacks, and
distractions that seek to scatter their focus.

Lord, I pray that Your Spirit anoints their words, actions, and
decisions, equipping them to minister with supernatural
effectiveness. Let Your flock know the love of God through their
shepherds, experiencing restoration, encouragement, and
abundant provision. Let no sheep remain lost due to lack of care or
guidance.

Father, may Your shepherds exercise patience, compassion, and
endurance, becoming living examples of Christ's heart for the

sheep. Let them rejoice in each soul restored, each life transformed, and each heart brought closer to You.

I decree that Your flock shall flourish under the guidance of Your shepherds, that Your Church shall thrive, and that every minister who seeks Your glory shall bear eternal fruit in abundance.

In Jesus' name, Amen.

DAY 24

SHEPHERD'S PROVISION

"The Lord is my shepherd; I shall not want. He makes me lie down in green pastures; he leads me beside still waters. He restores my soul; he leads me in the paths of righteousness for his name's sake. Yea, though I walk through the valley of the shadow of death, I will fear no evil; for you are with me; your rod and your staff comfort me. You prepare a table before me in the presence of my enemies; you anoint my head with oil; my cup runs over. Surely goodness and mercy shall follow me all the days of my life; and I will dwell in the house of the Lord forever."
— Psalm 23:1-6 WEB

O Lord of all shepherds, I lift before You my pastor and all ministers entrusted with the care of Your flock. I proclaim that they shall experience Your abundant provision, guidance, and protection as they shepherd Your people. May they lead with confidence, courage, and compassion, drawing from the green pastures of Your Word and the still waters of Your Spirit.

Heavenly Father, restore their souls, renew their vision, and empower them to walk steadfastly in paths of righteousness. Let them minister with authority and humility, guiding the flock safely through every trial and danger. Protect them from spiritual attack, discouragement, and weariness, and let Your anointing flow freely upon their lives.

Lord, may every shepherd experience the overflow of Your blessings, the joy of seeing souls restored, and the fulfillment of Your promises in their ministries. Let goodness and mercy follow them, and let their leadership bring peace, growth, and revival to Your Church.

Father, equip them to serve faithfully, providing nourishment, counsel, and protection to every member of their flock. May Your presence be their constant guide, their comfort, and their strength, enabling them to shepherd with excellence and love.

I decree that Your ministers shall dwell securely in Your house forever, their ministries fruitful, their hearts steadfast, and their labors rewarded in Your kingdom.

In Jesus' name, Amen.

DAY 25

TENDER SHEPHERD

"He will feed his flock like a shepherd; he will gather the
lambs with his arm, and carry them in his bosom; he will
gently lead those that are with young."
— Isaiah 40:11 WEB

O Lord God, Compassionate Shepherd, I lift up my pastor and all
those who lead Your Church. I declare that You will empower them
to shepherd tenderly, gathering the weak, the young, and the weary
with loving arms. Let every minister operate in gentleness, wisdom,
and strength, reflecting Your tender heart toward Your flock.

Almighty Father, may they lead with care, feeding the spiritual
needs of the flock, restoring those who are lost, and carrying the
burden of the weary with patience and compassion. Protect them
from burnout, opposition, and distraction, and let Your Spirit
continually renew their strength, courage, and vision.

Lord Jesus, fill them with discernment to guide, correct, and
nurture every soul in their care. Let their ministries be marked by
growth, healing, and transformation, as they emulate Your tender
leadership in every action, every word, and every decision.

Father, I prophesy that Your ministers shall be recognized for their
compassion, integrity, and sacrificial love. Let the flock thrive under
their care, growing in faith, maturity, and alignment with Your
heart. May Your glory be revealed in every shepherd who leads after
Your own heart.

O Lord, may the Church experience revival, renewal, and abundant life as Your shepherds faithfully lead, protect, and nurture the flock according to Your perfect will.

In Jesus' name, Amen.

WEEK 4: EMPOWERING AND PROTECTING SHEPHERDS

Leadership is a weighty responsibility, and shepherds face both visible and invisible battles. This week, our prayers are focused on empowering and protecting the leaders God has placed over His people. Every pastor, minister, and overseer must be strengthened in spirit, fortified in faith, and armed with the discernment to navigate spiritual, emotional, and practical challenges. We pray for the equipping of every shepherd to faithfully oversee their flock and fulfill God's calling without compromise or fear.

As you intercede, envision the shepherds standing strong, anointed and guided by God's Spirit. Pray for divine protection over their families, ministries, and personal lives, guarding them against the attacks of the enemy and the pressures of the world. Declare that every effort to destabilize their leadership will fail and that God's favor will surround them like a shield. Ask for supernatural wisdom, endurance, and courage to sustain them in the daily demands of shepherding.

We also lift up their spiritual growth, praying that their intimacy with God deepens daily and that they remain firmly rooted in His Word. Ask God to fill them with creativity in ministry, clarity in teaching, and passion in service. Pray that their lives reflect Christ's character, that they lead by example, and that their influence multiplies across communities, nations, and generations.

This week, expect breakthrough for every leader under intercession. Declare that their ministries flourish, their hearts remain steadfast, and their labor produces eternal fruit. Pray that the Church, under these shepherds, experiences growth, unity, and revival. By the close of this week, the shepherds will emerge strengthened, protected, and fully empowered to shepherd God's people with wisdom, grace, and courage.

DAY 26

FAITHFUL SHEPHERDS OF ISRAEL

He chose David his servant, and took him from the sheepfolds; he brought him from following the ewes that had young, to shepherd Jacob his people, and Israel his inheritance. He fed them with integrity of heart; with skillfulness he guided them.
— Psalm 78:70-72 WEB

O Great Shepherd of Israel, I lift up Your chosen servants, the pastors and ministers You have set over Your people. I declare that, as David was chosen from the sheepfolds, so You have selected them according to Your perfect wisdom and divine counsel. I pray that You anoint their hearts with unwavering integrity, that every decision they make and every step they take will reflect Your righteousness and glory. May they shepherd Your flock with skill, discernment, and tender compassion.

Lord, let Your Spirit grant them wisdom to guide, understanding to teach, and courage to lead even in the midst of opposition. Protect their hearts from weariness and discouragement, and renew their strength daily so that they may not falter under the weight of responsibility. May Your wisdom flow through them, bringing life, growth, and unity to every congregation and ministry they serve.

I pray for their families and personal lives, that You would surround them with peace, protection, and provision. Shield them from the attacks of the enemy who seeks to scatter, wound, or hinder the work of Your Kingdom. Empower them to remain steadfast, faithful, and diligent in every task You entrust to them.

Father, raise up an army of laborers who will support, uphold, and pray for these shepherds. Let them feel Your presence as a mantle of authority, guiding their footsteps and sustaining them through every trial. Strengthen their hearts to trust wholly in You, and to shepherd Your people with a heart that mirrors Yours.

O Lord, may their ministries bear fruit for generations to come, as they lead with Your heart, inspire with Your Spirit, and teach with Your truth. May they never grow weary in doing good, but always rejoice in the harvest of souls they bring into Your Kingdom. In Jesus' name, Amen.

DAY 27

GUARDIANS OF THE FLOCK

Take heed to yourselves, and to all the flock, among which
the Holy Spirit has made you overseers, to shepherd the
church of God which he purchased with his own blood. I
know that after my departing grievous wolves will enter in
among you, not sparing the flock.
— Acts 20:28-31 WEB

O Lord God, Almighty Protector of Your Church, I pray over the
shepherds You have appointed to lead Your people. I declare that
every overseer, pastor, and minister who stands in Your service is
divinely equipped and shielded by Your Spirit. Let the anointing of
the Holy Spirit empower them with vigilance, discernment, and
courage to guard the flock entrusted to them, for the enemy prowls
seeking to destroy, scatter, and deceive.

Father, strengthen them to lead with unwavering faithfulness,
keeping their hearts pure, their motives righteous, and their vision
fixed upon You. Protect them from hidden snares, from wolves who
come in guise of truth, and from all forms of spiritual sabotage. May
Your divine wisdom illuminate every decision and every word they
speak, ensuring that Your people are guided, healed, and spiritually
nourished.

Lord, infuse their spirits with endurance, perseverance, and joy as
they labor for Your Kingdom. Let the weight of responsibility never
crush their hearts, but rather mold them into leaders who

exemplify Christlike patience, courage, and humility. May their lives reflect Your glory, drawing multitudes into Your fold through their faithful service.

I pray, O God, that You surround them with godly counsel, steadfast allies, and intercessors who uphold them in prayer. Protect their families, strengthen their ministries, and grant them supernatural insight to anticipate and thwart every scheme of the enemy. Let them shepherd with wisdom, justice, and love, serving as models of integrity and devotion.

O Lord, cause their ministries to flourish, their hearts to burn with passion for Your glory, and their labor to yield abundant fruit for Your Kingdom. Let the flock they shepherd thrive under their guidance, experiencing growth, peace, and divine provision. In Jesus' name, Amen.

DAY 28

ENDURING IN THE MINISTRY

I charge you in the presence of God and of Christ Jesus, who will judge the living and the dead, and by his appearing and his kingdom: Preach the word; be ready in season and out of season; reprove, rebuke, exhort, with all patience and teaching.
— 2 Timothy 4:1-5 WEB

O Sovereign Lord, Author and Perfecter of our faith, I lift up Your ministers, pastors, and shepherds. I declare that they shall stand firm in every season, unshaken by opposition, temptation, or discouragement. Equip them to preach the Word with power, clarity, and conviction, reaching hearts and transforming lives. May they labor faithfully, diligently, and passionately, never growing weary, and always filled with Your Spirit.

Father, grant them discernment to know when to correct, when to exhort, and when to encourage, applying Your truth with grace and precision. Let patience and understanding guide their interactions, and let their teaching bear fruit in the hearts of Your people. Protect them from weariness, fear, or compromise that seeks to diminish their calling.

O Lord, establish their hearts in righteousness, fill them with courage, and strengthen their faith. Let every challenge they face refine them, deepen their reliance on You, and enhance their effectiveness in shepherding Your flock. Surround them with Your angels, defend them from every assault, and remove every obstacle placed by the enemy.

I pray, Heavenly Father, that their ministries flourish, that their lives exemplify Your holiness, and that their labors result in enduring spiritual growth for the congregation. Let Your wisdom, power, and love flow through them, bringing healing, guidance, and revelation to every soul they touch.

May the reward of their labor come forth abundantly, as You crown them with honor, joy, and peace, strengthening them to fulfill their calling to the glory of Your name. In Jesus' name, Amen.

DAY 29

HOLY LEADERSHIP EXEMPLIFIED

If anyone aspires to the office of overseer, he desires a good work. Therefore an overseer must be above reproach, the husband of one wife, temperate, sensible, respectable, hospitable, apt to teach; not given to wine, not violent, not greedy of filthy lucre; but gentle, not quarrelsome, not covetous; one who rules well his own house, having his children in submission with all dignity; for if a man does not know how to rule his own house, how will he take care of the church of God?
— 1 Timothy 3:1-7 WEB

O Lord, God of order and holiness, I lift up Your servants who aspire to shepherd Your people. I declare that every pastor, elder, and overseer shall embody integrity, temperance, and godly leadership. May their character reflect Your righteousness, their homes be sanctuaries of peace, and their families examples of submission, love, and dignity.

Father, anoint them with wisdom, humility, and discernment, equipping them to guide Your flock with gentleness and justice. Protect them from greed, violence, and pride, and cultivate in them hearts that serve rather than seek personal gain. May they be hospitable, teachable, and steadfast in faith, setting the highest standard for spiritual leadership.

Lord, strengthen them to withstand trials, opposition, and temptation. Let Your Spirit continually refine their character, deepen their understanding, and empower their ministries. May their leadership draw many into the knowledge of Christ, establishing Your Kingdom and glorifying Your name.

I pray for their health, both spiritual and physical, and for their families to flourish as models of godly living. Surround them with wise counselors, supportive communities, and abundant grace to sustain them in every season of ministry.

O Heavenly Father, may these shepherds lead with Your heart, protect Your flock diligently, and teach Your Word faithfully, bringing growth, unity, and revival wherever they labor. In Jesus' name, Amen.

DAY 30

CHRIST-CENTERED TEACHING

Him we proclaim, admonishing every man, teaching
every man with all wisdom, that we may present every
man complete in Christ.
— Colossians 1:28-29 WEB

O Lord Jesus, Great Teacher and Chief Shepherd, I lift up every
pastor and minister engaged in the work of discipleship and
teaching. I declare that they shall proclaim Christ with clarity,
power, and compassion, bringing every believer into fullness and
maturity in You. May their words be inspired by Your Spirit and
rooted in Your truth, shaping hearts and transforming lives.

Father, empower them with wisdom and discernment, enabling
them to teach with patience, insight, and authority. Strengthen
them to endure fatigue, opposition, and distraction, that they may
remain steadfast in presenting every soul complete in Christ. Let
Your Spirit flow through every sermon, lesson, and counsel,
bringing conviction, encouragement, and revival.

Lord, protect them from discouragement, false doctrines, and
spiritual attack. Let their hearts remain humble, their motives pure,
and their ministries fruitful. Surround them with godly counsel,
prayer partners, and communities that uphold and encourage
them.

I pray for their families, physical health, and emotional well-being,
that they may serve without hindrance and reflect Christ's

character in all areas of life. May the labor of their hands bear eternal fruit for Your Kingdom and glorify Your name.

O Lord, let every shepherd faithfully teach, faithfully lead, and faithfully love, bringing Your people into the abundant life that You promised. In Jesus' name, Amen.

DAY 31

WISE STEWARDSHIP

Know well the condition of your flocks, and pay attention
to your herds; for riches are not forever, nor a crown for
all generations.
— Proverbs 27:23-27 WEB

O Lord, Divine Shepherd and Provider, I lift up Your ministers and
pastors who are entrusted with the care of Your people. I declare
that they shall shepherd with wisdom, diligence, and discernment,
knowing well the condition of their congregations and attending to
every need with skill and love. May they recognize that every soul
is precious and that their leadership bears eternal significance.

Father, anoint them with insight and understanding, that they may
make wise decisions, manage resources faithfully, and nurture
every individual under their care. Protect them from distraction,
greed, and complacency, and empower them to lead with integrity,
humility, and compassion.

Lord, strengthen their hearts to persevere through challenges,
opposition, and seasons of trial. May they remain vigilant, attentive,
and faithful, reflecting Christ in every aspect of their stewardship.
Let Your Spirit guide every word, action, and plan, ensuring the
growth, health, and prosperity of Your flock.

I pray for divine provision, protection, and guidance over their
families, ministries, and personal lives. May their labor yield

eternal fruit, and may their example inspire future generations of shepherds who walk in Your truth.

O Lord, let them shepherd with Your heart, act with Your wisdom, and serve with Your love, bringing Your people into fullness and Your glory into every ministry. In Jesus' name, Amen.

EPILOGUE

As we close this 31-day journey of intercession, I want to remind you that the work of praying for shepherds does not end here. The Church is a living, breathing organism, and the leaders God has placed over His people continue to face battles—some visible, many unseen. Your prayers have not been in vain. Every declaration, every prophetic petition, and every Scripture lifted in faith has been recorded in heaven and will bear fruit according to God's perfect timing.

Now, you are called to move from this structured season of prayer into a lifestyle of intercession. Let the burden for shepherds become a permanent imprint on your heart. Continue to pray with passion, clarity, and authority, remembering that your voice is part of the divine chorus that sustains, protects, and empowers those who shepherd God's flock. Where there is prayer, there is protection. Where there is intercession, there is strength. And where there is persistence, there is victory.

Do not underestimate the power of your prayers. Pastors who are discouraged, exhausted, or under attack are strengthened by unseen hands lifted in persistent prayer. Ministers who face deception, division, and fatigue are fortified by those who stand in the gap. You have joined a spiritual movement that aligns heaven's resources with the needs of God's shepherds, ensuring that His people are nurtured, guided, and preserved.

As you step forward, continue to declare God's wisdom, protection, and empowerment over the shepherds in your life and across the global Church. Remind yourself daily that intercession is a divine privilege—a partnership with God in the advancement of His Kingdom. Let this be the beginning of a lifetime of prophetic intercession, a mantle you carry willingly, faithfully, and with unwavering expectation.

May every shepherd you have prayed for be strengthened, encouraged, and renewed. May their ministries flourish and their lives be surrounded by divine favor. And may your heart continue to beat in rhythm with God's, ever burdened for those who lead His people.

In Jesus' name, Amen.

ENCOURAGE OTHERS WITH YOUR STORY

If this prayer guide has strengthened your faith, deepened your intercession, or helped you stand in the gap, would you consider leaving a short review on Amazon? Your feedback not only encourages others but also helps more believers discover this resource and join in the prayer movement. Every review—just a few sentences—makes a difference. Thank you for being part of this movement.

MORE FROM PRAYERSCRIPTS

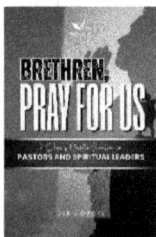

"BRETHREN, PRAY FOR US" SERIES

Brethren, Pray for Us:

31 Days of Prophetic Intercession for Pastors and Spiritual Leaders

They pray for us. But who prays for them?

Shepherds After My Heart:

31 Days of Prophetic Intercession for Raising Godly Shepherds and Flocks After God's Own Heart

Pastors, ministers, and spiritual leaders pour out daily to feed, guide, and protect the flock of God—but who stands in the gap for them?

Advancing the Word of God:

31 Days of Prophetic Intercession to See God's Word Multiply, Prevail, and Transform Lives

What if your prayers could push the Gospel forward, strengthen weary pastors, and open doors for God's Word to multiply across the nations?

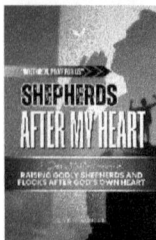

Command Your Morning:

30 Days of Prayers and Declarations to Seize Your Day and Shape Your Destiny

There is a battle over every morning—and every believer must choose to either drift into the day or command it.

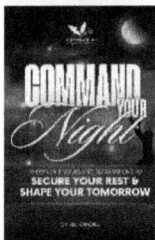

Command Your Night:

30 Days of Prayers and Declarations to Secure Your Rest and Shape Your Tomorrow

Every night is a spiritual battlefield—what you do before you sleep can determine the course of your tomorrow.

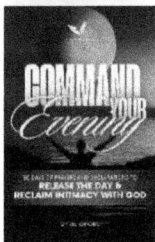

Command Your Evening:

30 Days of Prayers and Declarations to Release the Day and Reclaim Intimacy with God

There is a battle over every transition—and evening is one of the most spiritually neglected.

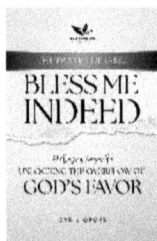

Bless Me Indeed:

Unlocking the Overflow of God's Favor

What if you could activate God's favor in your life today and walk in blessings that surpass your wildest expectations?

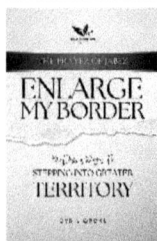

Enlarge My Border:

Stepping Into Greater Territory

Do you feel like you're living beneath your full potential? Do limitations, setbacks, and invisible barriers keep you from stepping into all God has promised? It's time to lift your cry for enlargement.

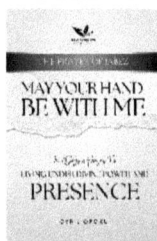

May Your Hand Be With Me:

Living Under Divine Power and Presence

What happens when the mighty hand of God rests upon your life? Doors open that no man can shut. Strength rises where weakness once prevailed. Guidance comes in the midst of confusion, and protection surrounds you in every battle.

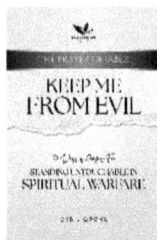

Keep Me From Evil:

Standing Untouchable in Spiritual Warfare

What if the enemy's plans could never touch you or your family? Imagine walking through life completely protected, untouchable, and victorious—no matter what schemes are formed against you.

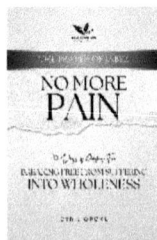

No More Pain:

Breaking Free from Suffering into Wholeness

Have you been carrying the weight of sorrow, disappointment, or hidden wounds for far too long? Do cycles of pain seem to repeat in your life, your marriage, or your family?

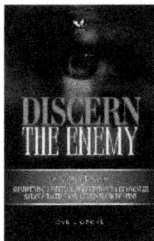

Discern the Enemy:

Sharpening Spiritual Perception to Recognize Satan's Tactics and Guard Your Destiny

The greatest danger is not the enemy you can see—it is the one you cannot. Can you recognize the enemy before he strikes?

Disarm the Enemy:

Stripping Satan of Weapons and Influence Through the Power of Christ

Are you tired of feeling like the enemy has the upper hand in your life? It's time to take back your ground, silence the lies of darkness, and walk in the unstoppable authority of Christ.

Destroy the Enemy:

Breaking Strongholds and Cancelling Evil Works by God's Authority

Are you tired of living under the weight of unseen battles? It's time to rise up and destroy the enemy's works in your life.

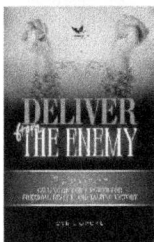

Deliver from the Enemy:

Calling on God's Power for Freedom, Rescue, and Lasting Victory

Break free from spiritual attacks and experience God's mighty deliverance in every battle.

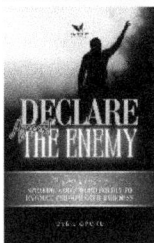

Declare Against the Enemy:

Speaking God's Word Boldly to Enforce Triumph Over Darkness

What if you could silence the enemy's schemes, protect your family, and walk boldly into every God-ordained assignment with unshakable authority?

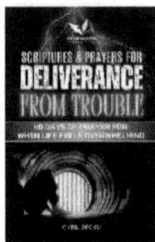

Scriptures & Prayers for Deliverance from Trouble:

40 Days of Prayer for When Life Feels Overwhelming

Are you walking through a season where life feels heavy and your prayers feel weak?

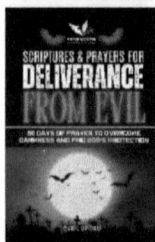

Scriptures & Prayers for Deliverance from Evil:

50 Days of Prayer to Overcome Darkness and Find God's Protection

When darkness presses in, how do you pray?

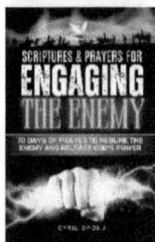

Scriptures & Prayers for Engaging the Enemy:

70 Days of Prayer to Rebuke the Enemy and Release God's Power

You weren't called to run from the battle—you were anointed to win it.

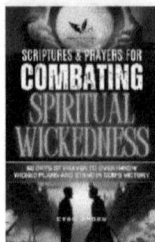

Scriptures & Prayers for Combating Spiritual Wickedness:

50 Days of Prayer to Overthrow Wicked Plans and Stand in God's Victory

Are you facing opposition that feels deeper than the natural? You're not imagining it—and you're not powerless.

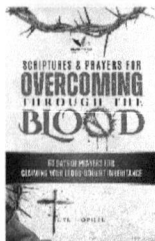

Scriptures & Prayers for Overcoming Through the Blood:

60 Days of Prayers for Claiming Your Blood-Bought Inheritance

You were never meant to fight sin, fear, or Satan in your own strength.

Standing in the Gap for Covenant Awakening:

30 Days of Prayer for National Repentance, Righteous Leadership & God's Sovereign Rule

What if your prayers could help turn the tide of a nation?

Standing in the Gap for Divine Defense:

30 Days of Prayer for National Guidance, Guarding & Glory

When the foundations of a nation feel as if they're shaking, prayer is the strongest fortress you can build.

Standing in the Gap for National Healing:

40 Days of Prayer for Reconciliation, Righteousness, and Restoration

What if your prayers could help heal a nation? What if God is waiting for someone—like you—to stand in the gap?

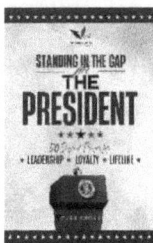

Standing in the Gap for The President:

50 Days of Prayer for Leadership, Loyalty, and Lifeline

When a nation's leader is under spiritual siege, will you answer the call to stand in the gap?

Pardon Through the Blood:

60 Days of Prayers for Total Forgiveness and Freedom

Guilt is a prison. The blood of Jesus holds the key.

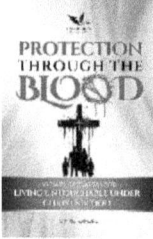

Protection Through the Blood:

60 Days of Prayers for Living Untouchable Under Christ's Blood

You are not helpless. You are not exposed. You are covered—completely—by the blood of Jesus.

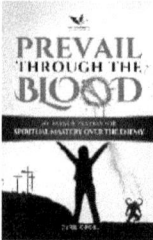

Prevail Through the Blood:

60 Days of Prayers for Spiritual Mastery Over the Enemy

What if every scheme of the enemy against your life could be dismantled—by one unstoppable weapon?

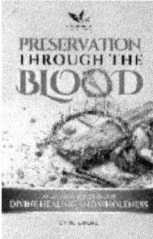

Preservation Through the Blood:

60 Days of Prayers for Divine Healing and Wholeness

Unlock Lasting Healing and Wholeness Through the Blood of Jesus

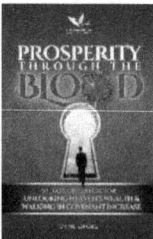

Prosperity Through the Blood:

60 Days of Prayers for Unlocking Heaven's Wealth and Walking in Covenant Increase

You were redeemed for more than survival—you were redeemed to prosper.

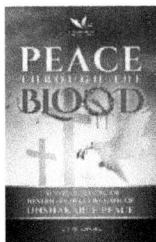

Peace Through the Blood:

60 Days of Prayers for Resting in the Covenant of Unshakable Peace

Are you ready to silence every storm of the mind, heart, and home—once and for all?

www.ingramcontent.com/pod-product-compliance
Lightning Source LLC
Chambersburg PA
CBHW062018040426

42447CB00010B/2044